PEDRO BRANCO

THE VOLATILITY TRADING PLAN

SAFELY SHORT VOLATILITY WITH OPTIONS PROVEN STRATEGIES AND PROPER RISK MANAGEMENT

First edition

Contents

III. The Trade Plan

About the Author

Pedro Branco has been an entrepreneur, an options trader, and a business consultant for more than fifteen years. He started trading stocks about twenty years ago but moved to options trading more than ten years ago. He started to trade stock options and then moved to index options. About four years ago, he started to research volatility properties and instruments, began to trade volatility ETNs, and focused his trades on this asset class. Due to his knowledge about options and searching for trading with consistency, he started to develop strategies using options that fit his risk level. Options are flexible instruments that provide better risk management opportunities to protect gains (and limit losses) if used wisely.

Currently, he exclusively trades in volatility, using VXX options. He is also an instructor at Udemy, transferring his knowledge and experience by teaching students how to properly manage options positions risk and implement his techniques, including one-on-one lessons. He teaches options strategies and has developed strategies on volatility. **Having bought this book, you can access any of his courses at his own website** www.myoptionsedge.com **(use links below).** Additionally, you can ask any question about volatility trading or request a mentorship program with one-on-one classes (pedro.branco.vol@gmail.com). He welcomes interaction with other people.

Currently, his four courses are some of the top ranked in "financial trading":
1. The Easiest Options Strategy
2. Beginner Level Options Strategy
3. The Croc Trade
4. The Volatility Surf Trade

In February 2020, after some requests from several students, he is posting his account and trades (with screenshots / full disclosing) which you can follow at https://www.myoptionsedge.com/follow-my-trades. His goal is to reach an annual profitability of 40% - 50%!

Aknowledgments

To my family for supporting me all these years.

To all the traders whom I've gathered knowledge from and who've inspired me to develop safer and consistent strategies.

To Udemy, which made it possible for me to reach several students who are eager to learn how to trade and who challenge me with new ideas.

Learn from Your Errors!

Always be prepared for the unexpected!

When It All Began

About twenty years ago, working as a management consultant, I was appointed to an energy industry (natural gas distributor) project in a leading company in Europe. At that time, local prices of crude and related energy products were increasing, and we had to support the client company with risk coverage approaches to improve the big client's pricing offer. This was my first contact with derivatives, and I became amazed with the flexibility they give.

After a couple of years, I started to research stock options and related strategies. Eventually, I opened my first options account at a newly created independent brokerage firm specializing in options trading, which had a powerful options-trading platform. Surely, you've heard about it—ThinkorSwim, years later bought by TD Ameritrade. I still use them as my preferred analysis tool to evaluate options positions and risk parameters, although I moved to another options-specialized brokerage firm with lower commissions.

At that time, I didn't succeed to be consistent. I wasn't focused. I had no strategy. I didn't know how to properly manage risk of my overall positions. I was more of a gambler than an investor or a trader. My first options account was blown in about three months! In a nutshell, I wasn't prepared for trade options.

Two more years later, I again started to research options trading and discovered index options strategies. I was now focused on not blowing up the account and on managing risk. I tested iron condors and broken wing butterflies in index options (mainly, SPX). But when I started to trade live, the market was very choppy, and it was hard to get profits in that environment, with so many adjustments. Also, I didn't understand that being out of the market could be a good trading strategy!

Again, I wasn't successful in trading and, upon reaching my loss level, withdrew the funds from my brokerage account and gave up trading options. Although the failed attempt was painful and demotivating, it provided me with a takeaway, as we always learn from any experience (either bad or good): I increased my knowledge and experience while trading options with focus on protecting capital, avoiding big losses, and understanding overall positions' risk.

Still, I was blaming myself. It was twice now that I had lost some money. Perhaps, I thought, the launched business wasn't good enough and led to losses. Like any startup business, trading is hard! Indeed, if it were easy, everyone would be gaining a lot of money very quickly. And for someone to gain, someone else must lose. Reality shows that most retail traders lose their hard-earned money.

Discovery of Volatility as a Tradeable Asset

One simple thing that intrigued me was VIX, the Cboe Volatility Index, and the way to trade it. If you look at its chart (Fig. ??), you can easily understand that it is very different from any stock chart. Of course, there are peaks. But mostly, VIX is below a certain value (e.g., 30) about 90 percent of the time and usually retracts to its "normal" values every so often. So perhaps, I thought, an opportunity exists to sell it when it is high enough...

In 2014, I started to research volatility issues and discovered a well-known article, "Easy Volatility Investing" by Tony Cooper.[1] The article transformed my understanding of the ways how trading this asset class can be conducted. Upon making this discovery, I continued to search the web, interact with other traders who had interest and experience in trading volatility opportunities, and discuss new models on how to invest in volatility.

In early 2015, markets were calm, contango was in place, and I started to invest directly in XIV, a former well-known short-volatility ETN. Things were good, investment was growing fast, and I went on vacation with my family in August. Long position was in place until we went to lunch and I connected to hotel Wi-Fi to see

---

[1]   <http://www.naaim.org/wp-content/uploads/2013/10/00R_Easy-Volatility-Investing-+-Abstract-Tony-Cooper.pdf>.

the markets. And bang, what a big surprise! Markets were crashing, volatility skyrocketed, and XIV lost half of its value in about a week. I was petrified!

When I came back home, I decided to understand what happened. A few weeks later, I decided to buy more XIV to average down the price paid and wait for contango to kick in and recover the losses. About a year later, the position entered in green territory and turned out to be a winner. Looking back, I think I was very lucky with that trade!

In 2017, I continued to apply this strategy—buying when volatility increased and the ETN had a price drop and then waiting for the markets to recover. A lot of money came in! During this process, I recovered all my past knowledge in options trading and started to apply it to volatility ETNs. Applying the leverage of options, I could invest less money in order to obtain better profitability.

Again, I started to research and found a very profitable way of selling VXX verticals at specific points in time at certain *Deltas*. (Don't worry if you don't understand these terms. I'll explain them later in the book.). Money started to come in. I used the winnings to put more money at risk. Thus compounding my investments allowed me to bring in even more money. I was overwhelmed, as I discovered something very profitable.

Then came February 2018 and brought something I'd never experienced. Not even in August 2015. Volatility went to stratosphere. XIV died. Was I ever glad that I had closed those direct positions! All my gains turned into losses. In VXX options verticals, I lost about 70 percent! I was expecting volatility to retrace faster and added other verticals. I chose not to stick to my trade plan: to enter only when contango is in place and closing positions are at a certain price level. Also, at that time, I wasn't protecting my account with hedges. Once again, I was the one who brought this misfortune upon myself by ignoring my past errors, becoming greedy, and being a gambler, not an investor!

Why This Book?

After my second disaster, in February 2018, I felt the need to share my knowledge and (both positive and negative) experience and give others an opportunity to earn some extra money or to live from trading. I started by launching a video course at Udemy, which was met with encouraging comments and reviews from several students. In response to the increased demand, I launched other courses. This book is another way to share my trading knowledge and strategies that you can apply.

I've read a lot of books about options trading. They all teach you the basics. Some describe in high detail all the strategies that you can apply. Others give you the math and the complexities of options trading. But none of them (at least, I didn't find any) teach you how to trade in a real market environment! To use a metaphor, they teach you what a fishing pole is and how to put the bait onto the hook. However, they don't tell you where to fish and how to cast the line.

I am not saying that those books aren't good. They are, because you need to understand how a vertical or an iron condor behaves with price and volatility changes and how to properly adjust. But they don't give you a **trade plan**. It seems that real consistent traders have something to hide. But I wrote this book to share my experience in trading volatility with a proper trade plan, focusing on what matters—the practical side of trading. That's why, the last section is mainly the trade plan that you can actually put into practice. <u>You can copy it, print it, and follow trade directions.</u> Do it and you won't miss anything! You can read all the directions before your trading day. If you follow it, I can assure you that you'll be gaining profits in the long term.

Finally, at the time of writing, we are approaching the final trading day of the most liquid volatility ETN that I exclusively trade: VXX from Barclays Bank. It will be liquidated on January 30, 2019, and I want to pay tribute to its twenty years of trading. But don't worry! It'll be substituted by VXXB, which will be here for twenty more years. Both ETN structures are the same, buying front two months of VIX futures. **So, when analyzing the past, I will refer to VXX. But strategies description should be applied to VXXB as it will be the same as VXX. Only the name changes!**

Stock versus Volatility trading

Volatility is elastic! Know how to play with it.

Stock Investing

Often, when some consider investing and trading, their first thought is to look for a stock to buy, hoping its price goes up later. There is nothing wrong with this view if yours is a short-term perspective.

Others buy to own stocks for several years. This is the spirit of investing. It is even better to use a more sophisticated approach by diversifying risk and creating a portfolio of owned stocks. But how to select the stocks to own?

If you are an emotional investor, you probably use non-objective criteria and put some of your resources into buzz companies. If you are more rational, you probably look for company multiples, diversify among different sectors, etc. Conducting this analysis isn't easy. Various companies possess various profiles. Some, like Tesla (ticker: TSLA), are currently non-profitable but possess high future prospects (growth expectations). Others, like Coca-Cola (ticker: KO), are value stocks that deliver earnings but possess much lower growth perspectives.

Fundamental analysis alone doesn't explain or provide guidance for stock market investing success. Short-term stock price movements in particular are driven by sentiment, which translates into price variations dictated by offer and demand. Sales growth expectations drive sentiment and turn around the stock of a non-profitable company by making it valuable. For example, in Q3, 2018, Apple announced lower sales expectations for 2019 and a growing profit. Following the announcement, the stock tumbled about 7 percent in after-market.

To sum up, the price of a single stock is highly influenced by its sentiment, which affects its stock offer and demand, which makes it difficult to spot its long-term direction. This also means that owning an individual stock carries substantial risk.

Fig. 3.1 – Tesla (TSLA) price chart, 2018.

Both price charts (TSLA and TWTR) show the risk involved when owning a single stock, especially "tech stocks" where results are mostly in the future (high expectations). Company valuation models consider discounted future cash flows. (If you want to learn about company valuation, consider Aswath Damodaran's website, <http://pages.stern.nyu.edu/~adamodar/>, for comprehensive literature on the subject).

Fig. 3.2 – Twitter (TWTR) price chart, 2018.

Even a stock like Coca-Cola (KO) is pretty volatile. See the price chart below.

Fig. 3.3 – Coca-Cola (KO) price chart, 2018.

Additionally, an individual stock can lose a lot in a single day if there is any lawsuit against the company or its leader (e.g., Elon Musk in October 2018, when TSLA lost more than 15 percent in one day).

For active and professional traders, tracking their portfolio stocks and finding new ones is hard work. But they are professionals and reap their rewards accordingly. For individual retail traders, whose resources such as time, information access and its study, and abilities to learn new techniques are limited, the task becomes much more difficult. Most individual investors add stock to their portfolios, based on limited analysis. For them, the process is more a game than a rational decision.

Due to this difficulty and work involved in stock picking, investment banks created Exchange-Traded Funds (ETFs), where individual investors have an opportunity to choose between a basket of stocks that could track a market index like S&P 500 ETF (ticker: SPY) or Nasdaq 100 ETF (ticker: QQQ), or a sector like Technology (ticker: XLK), or simply a commodity like Gold (ticker: GLD). There are currently thousands of ETFs that have a certain strategy and trade like a stock. This strengthens the gap between professional investors and individual investors, and there are professional investors that use several ETFs to diversify risk even more, combining uncorrelated assets. Nevertheless, there is risk associated with ETF investing. However, its volatility is lower than individual stock investing, and a combination of ETF investing could be a good passive investment if combined to reduce volatility.

Why to Trade Volatility?

A fast answer could be given if you compare the following price chart of Fig. 3.4 of Cboe VIX Volatility Index with the price behavior of individual stocks.

Fig. 3.4 – Cboe Volatility Index (VIX) price chart, 2018.

There are other trading considerations mentioned later in this book, but the first one to be highlighted is the price behavior of VIX compared to individual stocks. The main observations are as follows (for direct comparison between stock charts, a one-year timeframe was chosen; for a four-year period, go to Fig. 4.1):

1. Most of the time, VIX price sits between the 13- and 20-point marks.
2. When the price increases, it usually increases violently, as there are volatility peaks.
3. Price above the 25-point mark isn't a common reading.
4. When the price goes down, it does so at a slower pace than when it explodes.

Like volatility of any asset, VIX has a property called *mean reversion* referred to and demonstrated by Tony Cooper in the aforementioned article. This means that when volatility is high, the stock price tends to decrease and move closer to its average. On the contrary, when volatility is low, the stock price tends to increase, also moving closer to its average.

This means that, somehow, volatility and hence VIX price behavior are more predictable than an individual stock. When it's above the 25-point mark, the price is under pressure to come down sooner or later. As we saw with individual stocks, many uncontrollable factors affect price variations in unpredictable fashion, making trading risky. But this doesn't mean that trading volatility isn't riskier than trading individual stocks! **A more predictable price movement doesn't reduce risk if trading is conducted in an unsafe fashion.**

Shorting Volatility Is Risky!

Shorting volatility is a risk trade, when hedging techniques aren't taken into consideration, to avoid being wiped out when volatility explodes. On February 18, 2018, the big spike seen on the VIX price chart above was so violent that one short volatility ETN—VelocityShares Daily Inverse VIX Short-Term Futures (ticker: XIV)—was shut down and another—Proshares Short VIX Short-Term Futures (ticker: SVXY)—suffered losses of 90 percent but still trades.

To sum up, the market in its normal state calls for the volatility level to be around its average. Extremes in volatility have lower duration. In Chapter 6, I analyze the VIX futures curve shape and its importance for our strategy. For now, you can remember that the normal state of volatility is in play most of the time (85 percent), which relates to the upward futures curve.

The Cboe VIX index: The Fear Gauge

Volatility takes the stairs down but the elevator up!

It all starts with this well-known fear indicator of the stock market—the Cboe Volatility Index (ticker: VIX). However, although it is well known, most people referring to it don't know much about it, what it means, or what it measures. Hence, a brief VIX introduction below.

VIX is a measure of the implied volatility of S&P 500 (ticker: SPX) options in a 30-day period. Implied volatility is different from historical volatility of an asset. The former is determined by the market price of option contracts—driving forces between buyers and sellers for each contract (and is one of the main drivers of options pricing). The latter is the risk observed by price movement of an asset and is directly related to its standard deviation. This means that an asset could have low historical volatility and high implied volatility in a given moment. Implied volatility is related to the expected (future) price movement of an asset. This discrepancy between historical and implied volatility is observed mainly prior to earnings announcements, where there is high implied volatility compared to historical volatility (especially in big tech companies).

But Cboe uses several option prices of SPX option chain to compute its value. SPX and the VIX have a negative correlation. There are also other related volatility indexes for other known indexes—e.g., Nasdaq 100 (ticker: NDX) or Russell 2000 (ticker: RUT) and Dow Jones Industrial Average (ticker: DJX)—with the same principles.

To sum up, VIX is based on option quotes that display the market's estimation of volatility of SPX for the next 30-day period.[2] In the case of a certain event where there is uncertainty or SPX starts to decline, market participants start to buy SPX Puts, and their implied volatility starts to increase. As a result, VIX also starts to raise its value. If SPX has a violent drop, VIX will also have a violent spike like the ones we observed in February 2018. On the other hand, when the market starts to recover from a recent correction, the following happens: uncertainty erodes, market participants start to sell their protection, VIX options implied volatility decreases, and VIX also decreases. Usually, volatility spikes are more violent than volatility contractions, as you may expect, due to strong buying pressure of options (for protection) when the market suddenly starts to fall.

Let's now move to the interpretation of VIX's value. Being the 30-day implied volatility of SPX, the VIX value states an annualized volatility of the broader market index and can be directly interpreted. When VIX is quoted at 15, it means SPX can move by 15 percent on either side in an annualized move over the next thirty days. This value can be used to compute the expected move of the market for smaller time frames.

We can compute the expected value in the next thirty days, using a simple formula: VIX Value / Square Root of 12.[3] In the example given, the expected move of SPX in the next month is 15 / SQRT(12) = 4.3%. Given the same rationale, we can also compute the expected move of the broader market index in one day. In this case, the formula changes the SQRT of 252 as the number of trading days. In our example, the expected daily move of SPX for the day is 15 / SQRT(252) = 0.9%.

But from a trading perspective, **how can VIX be traded?** The answer is very simple. **It can't!** VIX itself isn't a tradeable asset. In the following chapters, we discuss how to mimic VIX trading as well as how to safely trade volatility, especially when shorting it. As we can see in the following chart, it is like a beast that can be dormant but can also suddenly wake up and explode.

Fig. 4.1 – VIX chart, 2015–2018.

---

[2] No additional details will be given in this book as it includes some complex computations from SPX option chain and does not bring value from a trading perspective

[3] 12 refers to the number of months with an average of 30 days.

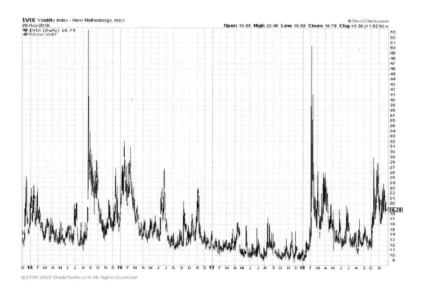

The only way to trade VIX is using derivatives and volatility ETNs:

- VIX futures (discussed in the next chapter)

- Options on VIX futures: for each future, there are options available. Be aware that for each expiry of VIX options, there are related VIX futures—not VIX itself—with the same expiry date! Therefore, calendar spreads with VIX options aren't available in some brokerages because each option of the calendar is from a different asset. (ex, in an SPX calendar it is sold a front month option at a certain strike price and bought a later expiration option at the same strike price - but both for the same asset: SPX; in the case of VIX calendars the bought and sold options at the same strikes refers to different assets: front and back months futures!);

- ETNs (Exchange-Traded Notes discussed in Chapter 7, with focus on VXX (and VXXB)).

Finally, Cboe launched other volatility indexes on SPX with several time frames. For example, VIX3M measures the volatility of SPX in a longer time frame, a three-month period (ninety days), measuring the implied volatility in longer-dated options on the broader market index. To compare, VIX9D is a short-term volatility index with a nine-day time frame, and it measures the SPX volatility for that period. Also, there are volatility indexes for the leading market indexes like Nasdaq 100 or Dow Jones Industrial Average, which can be monitored at the Cboe website, <http://www.cboe.com/products/vix-index-volatility/volatility-on-stock-indexes>.

VIX Futures Pricing Structure

If you expect the market to move one way, it will probably move the other.

VIX Futures Curve Dynamics

As discussed in the previous chapter, VIX isn't a tradeable asset. There are indirect but related ways to trade VIX, using some related products—namely, its futures market. Another way (discussed in the next chapter) is to use available volatility ETNs, which is more accessible to individual investors. To better understand the nature of these ETNs and the ways of trading them with an edge, it is useful to analyze the VIX futures market to see how the shape of its curve influences trading decisions.

Simply put, VIX futures can be seen (ignoring intrinsic variables that also impact their pricing) as estimation of where VIX will close on the future expiration date (where spot VIX and future will settle). VIX future price at any given expiration date reflects the equilibrium price from market participants to where VIX index will settle.

As with other futures markets, where there are several months forward, VIX futures prices can freely navigate above or below spot VIX, depending on bets from market participants that either can enter long or short trades. Vixcentral.com is one leading source of information of volatility-related parameters, including VIX futures curve (Fig. 5.1). The curve shape presented shows a normal state of the market where volatility is low. Usually, when volatility is lower the 15–16 mark, the curve has this growing shape. And this could be easily understood: As we go further in time, market uncertainty increases; hence, market participants are willing to pay higher value for volatility. In the example given in the figure below, if Spot VIX is quoted at 10 and there is about one week until December VIX future expiration, this future is likely to have a price closer to Spot VIX than March future where there about 3.5 month far out.

Fig. 5.1 – VIX futures price structure, beginning of December 2017, <www.vixcentral.com>

In the example above, all VIX futures are above spot VIX (also known as cash VIX). Hence, if someone buys the December future at 10.93, and at expiry date, the Spot VIX settles at 10.0 (let's assume this for simplicity), it will lose 0.93 per contract (x US$100 due to futures contract leverage). Futures are mainly used to hedge long market (SPX) positions, gaining from increase in volatility (covering losses from long market exposition), but also for speculation on volatility. But, as you understand, when someone buys VIX futures for protection, they must assume a cost—the cost of protection. On the contrary, someone that sold the same future would gain that lost amount (as this is a null sum market like the stock market)! Volatility buyers usually buy portfolio insurance, which like any other insurance, comes at a cost; Volatility sellers support buyers insurance policy by making it possible by being at the other side of the market. The red arrows pointing towards Spot VIX illustrate the "pressure" or the movement of the futures to settle at Spot VIX value.

When markets are calm, with low volatility, Spot VIX remains below the front month, and there is this negative "drift" towards it. Every day, futures and Spot VIX get closer to each other. The ratio between the front month future and Spot VIX is called **roll yield** and could be negative in calm/normal market conditions or positive if volatility is high after a market crash and VIX goes above front month future and the curve inverts. In Fig. 5.1 above, that ratio can be computed as follows:

roll yield = front month future price / spot VIX − 1 = 10.93 / 10.01 − 1 = 8.97% (which means that December future buyers should expect 8.97 percent loss until expiry date if VIX remains at 10.01)

This is defined as a yield because it may pay or cost a small amount every day as the futures price and the Spot VIX converge. The market isn't static, and VIX future pricing is the best way of predicting volatility from each moment to each expiry date in the futures chain.

Further analyzing the curve shape of Fig 5.1, given that the futures are aligned in a rising price, it is said to be in **contango**. This means that there is a positive ratio between the second month price and the first month price. This is also a very important measure, and it strongly impacts some ETN trading described in the following chapters. The contango level is also important and can be computed for each month interval. Here is its illustration for the two front months futures as these are used by majority of volatility ETNs. Again, it is a ratio similar to roll yield above.

contango = second month future price / first month future price − 1 = 12.32 / 10.93 − 1 = 12.72%

Usually, in normal market conditions, the ratio is positive and is said to be in contango. When markets crash, there is a volatility increase and the curve inverts. The ratio become negative and is said to be in **backwardation**.

In Fig. 5.2 below, there is an illustration of both concepts.

Fig. 5.2 – Illustration of roll yield (red shading) and contango (green shading) levels

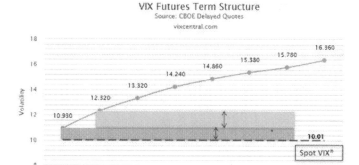

During a market crash, market participants rush to protect their portfolios and start to buy protective puts on SPX, which results in the increasing VIX Index. The example below illustrates the situation on February 6, 2018, when during the second day of very high volatility, VIX closed at about 30. As you can see, the futures curve inverted and is now pointing towards Spot VIX above (not included in the graph). Front month future has less than ten days to expiration, and market participants are expecting the VIX to end up a bit lower at the time of the expiration date (at 23.875).

Fig 5.3 – VIX futures pricing structure on February 6 during a market crash and volatility spike

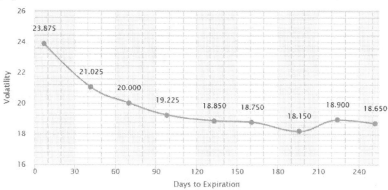

An additional characteristic of VIX and futures price is the rate of movement when a volatility event occurs. As these graphs show, Spot VIX reacts faster than its futures. On February 5, it had a low of 16.8 and a high of 38.8. The following day it had a low of 22.4 and a high of 50.3. This shows variations above 100 percent! Futures show lower variations because they lag the Spot VIX, and there is time premium between front month and spot VIX (obviously, if the volatility event would have been in an expiry front month day, the future would have also had similar violent moves). To sum up, the farther away the future expiration date is, the smoother movement or volatility is. In Fig 5.3 above, you can see that the second month is predicting a lower volatility value on the expiration date and a lower volatility value for the third month. And this is because volatility has mean reversion properties.

VIX Futures Term Structure over Time

In the previous section, we described the way the curve structure of VIX futures can assume two distinct shapes:

1. **Contango**: Where front month volatility is lower than following months and spot VIX is below the front month value (positive roll yield) — it has a growing shape (Fig 5.2)
2. **Backwardation**: When VIX spikes suddenly and the front future follows this movement and its price is above the second and following months also spikes and assumes a decreasing value shape (Fig. 5.3)

At this moment, we can consider the time variable into the equation of our volatility analysis and try to understand why we consider contango to be the "normal market state." Based on Fig 5.4 below illustrating the contango/backwardation (top graph) and roll yield (lower graph) levels in the past ten years, we can conclude the following:

1. Majority of time, in normal market conditions, which means volatility in a low state (<15), contango is in place. This occurs approximately 85 percent of the days. Sustaining short volatility strategies is very important (as it is discussed in the second part of this book).
2. Backwardation state occurs during low periods and mostly doesn't stay for too long. In this 10-year period, only in 2011 and 2015, it took some months to recover to normal contango condition. In February 2018, where there was one big volatility event, it took about two months to recover to contango.
3. Negative roll yield is highly correlated with backwardation, but due to its ratio (between spot VIX and front month), it is more elastic. Negative roll yield event takes less time to recover to positive roll yield.

Fig 5.4 – Contango level (blue line, top graph) and roll yield level (green line, lower graph), 2009–2018

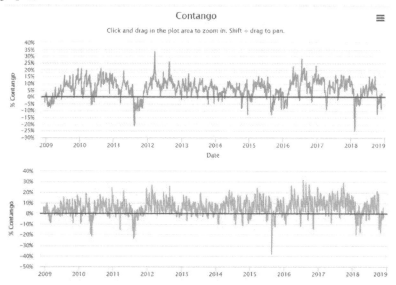

To sum up, volatility sellers could have trading opportunities to profit if they know the status of VIX futures structure and expected movement. In fact, market participants want to sell volatility when it's high (with futures in backwardation) that feeds the other side of buyers willing to protect their portfolios (buying side).

6

Volatility Exchange-Traded Notes (ETNs)

If you expect to earn 20 percent in a trade, consider paying for insurance, i.e., hedge your position.

As seen in the previous chapter, VIX isn't a tradeable asset. VIX futures and options are the related proxies that are available for trading with the characteristics described earlier through the use of ETNs. An ETN is a debt security that is backed by the credit rating of the issuer. The goal of an ETN is to replicate an investment strategy or performance of another investment vehicle. They are similar to Exchange-Traded Funds (ETFs), but instead of having assets that mimic the composition of an index, for example, they are a debt security (they have credit risk of the issuer) that mimic the performance of an index. In the ETFs, there are assets held, and hence the risk isn't associated with the financial institution that issues it but is related to the assets held.

There are several volatility-based ETNs to choose from. The full list can be obtained from ETF.com, <https://www.etf.com/channels/volatility-etfs>. On the top of liquidity list is VXX (**iPath® S&P 500 VIX Short-Term FuturesTM),** which was the first to be issued by Barclays Bank on January 30, 2009. This was the start of a new asset class: Volatility. After ten years of trading, it will reach maturity on January 30, 2019, and will be substituted by a newer version VXXB (**IPath® Series B S&P Short-Term FuturesTM**), also from Barclays, which started trading in early 2018. **This book is focused on analysis and trading on VXX that can be replicated in VXXB. Only the name changed. Its structure is exactly the same as VXX.**

Volatility ETNs trade like a stock, have a ticker, and some of them have issued options. The price of the VIX futures determines the Net Asset Value (NAV) of each ETN. Throughout the day, traders can buy and sell them and when NAV gets too far from the fair price, the market makers execute orders to correct the price. There are also long and short volatility ETNs and different leverage degrees, which can be used to pursue different strategies. They are shown in the following table.

Fig. 6.1 – Examples of volatility ETNs

Ticker	Issuer	Long/Short	Leverage	Options
VXX	Barclays	Long	1x	Yes
VXXB	Barclays	Long	1x	Yes
SVXY	Proshares	Short	0,5x	Yes
UVXY	Proshares	Long	2x	Yes
TVIX	Credit Suisse	Long	2x	No

Simply put, VXXB tries to mimic VIX daily variations on a 1:1 variation. SVXY is the opposite. It has an inverse relation with VIX, with softened variations (half due to its 0.5x leverage). Hence, if VIX increases by 5 percent, SVXY is expected to decrease by 2.5 percent. In fact, these variations between ETNs and VIX aren't exactly like described and are a bit softened, because their composition is based on VIX futures that also have daily variations lower than VIX itself.

It's important to understand that sometimes volatility ETFs don't move as expected by VIX movement. For example, VXX can go down while VIX is going up. The reason is the way these ETNs are implemented. In order to mimic VIX, these ETFs use VIX futures that are traded on Cboe, and this causes some unsuccessful parity due to the shape of the VIX futures curve. VXX (with VXXB following the same index strategy) is composed by VIX futures, as its goal is to gain exposure to the front two months of VIX futures. Every day, it invests in long positions of the first and second months. The balance between each month is adjusted daily along the month development. Barclays publishes the daily composition of VXX on its website under Index Components, <http://www.ipathetn.com/US/16/en/details.app?instrumentId=259118>. At the start of a cycle, just after the front month VIX future expires, the composition of the ETN is basically 100 percent long the second month (which now turned to be the front month) and 0 percent of the second month (former third month). The next day, the first month becomes 1/30 less relevant, and so on.

Fig 6.2 – VXX futures composition on November 30, 2018, taken from the iPath website. Front month expiry on December 18 on December 21; January 2019 expiry on January 15.

Index Components(as of 11/30/2018)

Index Components	Weightings %
CBOE VIX Future DEC 18	67.90%
CBOE VIX Future JAN 19	32.10%

Source: S&P Dow Jones Indices LLC, subject to change.

About one year after the launch of VXX, Cboe introduced options on this ETN. These options trade just like any other, and similarly each contract represents one hundred shares of VXX. Currently, they also haven't only monthly expiring options but also weeklies on this ETN, which are on the top liquidity list of traded assets.

Fig. 6.3 – Comparison of price movement of VXX and VIX, September–November 2018

Figure 6.3 shows a comparison of price movement of both VXX (left graph) and VIX (right graph) in a three-month period. As we can observe, both VXX and VIX are highly correlated, which means that both price variations are very similar. In fact, the intent of VXX is mainly to mimic VIX, and it is used to hedge long stock positions in short time frames (better intraday).

In periods of high volatility and VIX increases, VXX also increases. But if you look in more detail, there are "minor" differences that should be highlighted because they are very important. For instance, VXX peaked twice in October, and the first peak was lower than the second one. In the same period, VIX also peaked twice in October, but the first peak was higher than the second one. These differences occur because of the way VXX daily rebalances VIX futures. As described earlier, VXX is composed of two-month VIX futures that, in normal market conditions (structure in contango), lose time value until they reach spot VIX at expiration. This fact, as VIX futures converge to spot VIX, means that (1) a future contract with a lower price is being sold and (2) another future contract, with a higher price, is being bought as a movement of daily rebalancing. This activity results in the VXX not tracking the VIX with exactitude.

In the case of Figure 6.3, it was a period of higher volatility, and VIX futures were inverted and were in backwardation, which justifies the bigger second peak of VXX in comparison to VIX. But this graph shows a small timeframe. Figure 6.4 shows the VXX price evolution over the past four years, and the difference between it and the VIX graph in Fig. 4.1 is remarkable.

Fig. 6.4 – VXX price history, 2015–2018.

Over the long term, VXX decays in price. The chart period shows it peaking around US$580 in early 2015 and is currently trading near 34. It has a huge negative price behavior. VXX is also known by convexity, and contango and roll yield from VIX futures erase value from it. To compare, VIX has its peaks due to volatility explosions but is steady in the long run. If you remember, VXX is composed of a rolling percentage (along the month) of the two front months of VIX futures. Due to roll yield, VIX futures normally decay in value. Hence, both futures lose money, which also brings VXX to lose its value (when markets are in contango, their normal state).

This usually is referred to as a headwind for VXX; it's also a decaying factor for VXX price. On the other hand, when markets decrease and volatility is high—VIX futures structure in backwardation—VXX has a tailwind, and the price is pushed higher.

7

Which Side are You On?

You won't always be on the winning side!

When trading volatility, there are two options: (1) the "easiest" but scary and (2) the "other." Usually, volatility traders are on the selling side and the buyers are portfolio protectors. By now, you probably understand that buying volatility is a slow losing game. In fact, this is mostly true because buying VIX futures will have the roll yield drag, which is the cost of insurance that buyers are willing to pay to protect their portfolios. I don't know any trader that has a "pure" buy side volatility strategy who is willing to have a cost and who is expecting a "black swan" event to pay for a small monthly loss while being exceptionally profitable. By definition, black swan events are rare. It's like winning the lottery!

The short-volatility trading is "easier" to adopt, as it produces short-term income (when conditions are met). In a low-volatility environment, contango and roll yield are in place, and traders are cashing in on the loss of value of futures or ETNs. It's easy to become hypnotized by "easy" profits and increase exposition in an attempt to increase profits. During long periods of calm markets, like in 2017, high levels of contango were in place and short-volatility sellers were profiting high! But volatility is dormant only until it explodes! Then, all the "easy" profits are wiped out, and accounts end up with huge drawdowns. We shouldn't forget that even when the markets are closed (weekdays and weekends), futures can gap, and the next day we could have big losses! Remember, market trading is a null sum game: if one side wins, the other side loses!

Short volatility strategies should combine hedging positions to avoid huge losses in case of a volatility peak event, to prevent those losses. As you may understand, this insurance comes with a cost. Some hedging techniques that I apply are discussed in the next section and are to be applied to each strategy discussed. All strategies described include options, which are an instrument that is highly flexible when managing risk. This means that the structure of the strategy can be self-hedged. Hedged techniques can include *Delta* (directional risk) hedging with VIX calls, or more complex combinations to hedge against *Vega* (volatility risk), or even *Theta* risk (time decay of options). One of the simplest volatility hedges is using VIX Calls, but at the expense of time (*Theta* decay). If we want to reduce the effect of time decay, (*Theta* decay), it can be used VIX Call spreads instead.

But the most important thing about properly applying hedging techniques is to have them in place before any event. Otherwise, the desired protection effect won't be there. And we shouldn't forget that hedging also has a cost. It will reduce overall portfolio profitability (buying insurance has a cost), but in case of a sudden volatility explosion, you'll be glad to have those trades in place. You'll soften the overall position loss as well the gains. You should see hedging not as full portfolio protection but as a fraction of it. If you are fully hedged, the loss in the main position would be equal to the gains with the hedges.

8

Trade Management

You are an investor, not a gambler!

Before describing each trade and its profitability, I decided to describe how to have proper focus and how to trade consistently. This chapter is as important as the ones that describe the strategies and the trade plan. A good strategy (or a profitable one) isn't enough to deliver the desired results. Every trade comes with a risk; otherwise it would be a free lunch. Markets are liquid enough to turn these opportunities into difficulties. Therefore, it is necessary to have clear understanding of when to abandon a trade if it goes against what is expected (as well as when profit target is reached). I encourage you to use a trade spreadsheet to control entry and exit points. Do this in order to become less prone to emotions. When you enter a trade, know when to exit. **And more important: execute trade closing if those points are touched!** Open a new trade if (or when conditions are met). (It will be better positioned than the previous one.) When I started to trade, I had several losses because I expected the market to retract and—you guessed it—the market continued to do the opposite. You can imagine what happened. I increased my losses. So when you enter a trade, write down the exit points (either at a profit or a loss) and stick to it. **Don't try to guess the market. PERIOD!**

In essence, what I mean is if you want to trade to double your account in three months, you need to take huge risks. There is no other way. Besides, you need to gain a lot and lose a little. Currently, I am not this kind of trader. (Is this the profile of a trader?) When I started to trade, I made these rookie mistakes and lost an entire account. I also had huge winnings. But I had no idea what I was doing. I wanted big winnings. The only way to win big in a short period is to win the lottery. Like many others, I learned the hard way. Now I am focusing on consistency in the long term. I prefer to control my risk and target an average monthly return of 5 percent to 10 percent (with periodic losses). If I get 40 percent a year, I am satisfied. This means that I am doing the right thing. Manage risk and take profit from the market.

Traders' framework / Money Management

Money management is crucial for long-term capital appreciation and gaining profits. As discussed, exit points for each opened trade must be defined at opening to control losses and make the best usage of the invested capital. Even with a profitable trade, it is possible to better use capital if a closing date is approaching or the percentage of maximum profit is high enough. For example, if you are one week away and the trade has reached 70 percent of the maximum profit potential, why wait until the expiration time? Better to close and invest in a new trade that, for sure, will have lower risk. Last trading days, just before the options expiration, have increased *Gamma* risk, meaning *Delta* variations are highly pronounced (instrument price and *Delta* movements are highly sensitive for better and for worse). At this time, the best option is to take out profits, enter a new trade (if conditions are met), and be better positioned for the next period at a lower risk (underlying price movement).

Managing losses is crucial to achieve consistency. Fig. 8.1 compares three hypothetical traders with different trading profiles/outcomes and the respective outcomes needed to be profitable. Trader 1 has an average winning trade of US$50 and manages the losses to keep them equal to the winnings. He needs only a 60 percent win rate to turn his trade profitable in the long term. To compare, Trader 3 who wins US$25 per trade and loses US$100 per losing trade needs a higher than 80 percent win rate to gain profits. Keep this example in mind when trading!

As you can conclude, it is **more important to cut your losses than manage your winnings**. One big loss can ruin your whole account. So when your loss level is reached, act fast and close the trade. Don't try to guess whether the market goes back. Close the trade and move on. Even if the market retracts, don't blame yourself. Remember: Your goal is to profit in the long term! **Without being disciplined, you won't achieve the desired consistency**.

Fig 8.1 — Profitability comparison of three trader profiles.

	Trader 1	Trader 2	Trader 3
Avg Profitable trade (USD)	50	25	25
Avg Loosing trade (USD)	-50	-50	-100

Avg Win Rate	Expectancy		
80%	30	10	0
70%	20	2,5	-12,5
60%	10	-5	-25
50%	0	-12,5	-37,5
40%	-10	-20	-50

I understand that it could be difficult to have a losing trade. But the trading path in a certain period includes losing trades. The goal is to find a strategy that will give you an edge if the markets behave a certain way. If they behave in another way, it's better to move on to another strategy. And this book is about giving you the exact trade plan for higher-volatility and lower-volatility types of market.

You should have the mental attitude of a trader before you enter any trade, because two outcomes are possible: winning or losing. If a certain previously defined price or loss is reached, close the trade! If a certain previously defined profitability point or an expiry date is reached, close the trade! Remember that what counts is to achieve consistency in the long run. You are an investor, not a gambler!

Finally, depending on the level of risk of each trade, you should define the percentage of buying power allocated to it. For example, a short call vertical has more intrinsic risk than an unbalanced iron condor (see the following chapters) in VXXB, and hence, I wouldn't advise to have more than 5% percent of account allocated to the former strategy (with additional hedges). As for the latter strategy, 50 percent is an acceptable level due to its upside protection in case of volatility explosions.

Analyzing my past trading experience, I would say that it was unsuccessful because I didn't manage my losses. I couldn't let go off the lost trade. I was too greedy and kept waiting for the market to retract. Please, don't trade this way! Study well your trade plan (or the one that is given in this book) and stick to it! Don't guess which way the market is going to go. Control your overall risk. If you want to put a new type of trades into your live account, please test it first in a paper money account.

Final point: **Manage your losses, not your winnings!**

9

VXX Short-Term Price Analysis

When you open a trade, be prepared for the worst. Hedge!

As seen in the previous chapter, VXX will lose its value in the long run (see Fig. 6.4) due to its structure and the fact that VIX futures are in contango most of the time. But what about the short-term prognosis? Fig. 9.1 below shows a histogram of percentile variance of VXX over the following fifteen days (for the last three years). Two main conclusions may be drawn:

1. Majority of the time (above 70 percent), VXX will end at a lower point than the price on a given day.
2. There is about 10 percent of the time (not to be neglected!) when the price goes up more than 15 percent.

Such price behavior is confirmed by observing the VXX price graph: It has a negative slope but sometimes presents huge increases in price. With those in mind, some trades can be developed depending on market conditions and will be described in the next chapters.

Fig. 9.1 – VXX prices, fifteen-day histogram analysis.

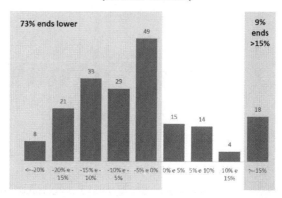

More analysis was conducted over a more extended period and timeframe, which led to similar conclusions. Obviously, if the price variation analysis considered an even more extended period (e.g., six months or one year), the percentage of days ending at a low point would be close to or even higher than 90 percent. For the sake of not having too much repetitive information, only one graph per short timeframe is included here.

10

The Easiest Volatility Options Strategy

Guessing the market direction is hard! I mostly fail trying to do it.

When I thought about writing this book, I intended to describe in detail my two main volatility strategies (described in the following chapters). Nevertheless, I wanted to find an easy way to learn a strategy by simply buying an option. This should be a good start for entry-level options traders.

But when I say it's "easy," it reflects non-complex options positions and easy-to-apply management guidelines, without any adjustments. Using backtesting software for non-complex options spreads from Capital Market Laboratories, <www.cmlviz.com>, and given the price properties (price erosion over time) of VXXB, it would be easy to think that by simply buying a put option, you would be getting a positive outcome. This would be totally true if options' decay didn't come into the equation. When buying any option (in this case, a put option), *Theta* is negative, which means that it'll basically lose value as time passes until its expiration date. Also, buying a put option will produce a negative *Delta* trade, which is in line with where we expect the VXXB price to move, meaning this is a directional play. This scenario would be similar to short directly the underlying (but without the high risk of a volatility spike producing huge negative returns as the loss is capped by the value of the price paid for the put option). This means that the trade will gain if the price decay of VXXB happens as fast as possible. Putting it all together, this trade will achieve a positive return only in case of a rapid price decay that offsets

---

4 Please refer to Chapter 17 for an understanding of option greeks.

Theta loss (time erosion of the put). In essence, we are saying that *Delta* (which measures the price movement) should be higher in absolute value than *Theta* (which measures the daily option value decay).

Theta options decay is higher in the last thirty days till expiration (DTE). In the last week, *Theta* decay increases abruptly, which we don't want for this type of strategy. So, we should focus on buying longer-dated options. Let's assume, as a starting point of this trade, the 60 DTEs option. (At this moment, I already know that it'll produce the best results). Now, we have the main drivers of the trade, and we can use a backtester to understand which put option to buy in that timeframe (i.e., which put option (at which *Delta*) produces the best results.)

Fig. 10.1 – Trade profile of VXXB put buying, with two lines: (1) t0 line (magenta) and (2) at expiry date (light blue line).

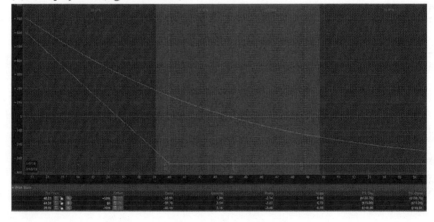

In Fig. 10.1, we can see that when VXXB price decays, the put option bought produces a positive return: Go along the magenta line—the line that represents profitability of the option at the date we are observing (t0 line) (the cyan line represents the profile of the put option at maturity). As we can see, the Greeks are aligned as required in this type of trade: *Delta* is negative and much more negative than *Theta*. Its ratio (*Delta/Theta*) is about 10. So, this is a directional trade as we designed it. If by next day, VXXB price drops to 40, there will be about US$145 gain with this trade, since we move to the left of the magenta line, but it will drop a bit due to *Theta* decay (maintaining volatility constant). It would be around US$148 if no *Theta* decay were in place (see the bottom right corner). To illustrate the effect of the *Theta* decay in this structure, see below how different both trade profiles are thirty days later, with only time being the factor.

Fig. 10.2 – VXXB put option thirty days later, with all other variables as constant (i.e., VXXB price, volatility, etc.)

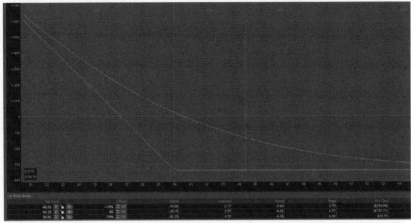

With no movement in price of VXXB, and after thirty days, the trade shows a US$137 loss due exclusively to *Theta*. Also, *Theta* decay value increases due to the approach of expiration where the last days have the most decay (bigger value in the Fig. 10.2 than in Fig.10.1).

Now that we've looked at the trade profile, let's move on to the backtesting outputs used to compare the profitability of buying a put option at different *Deltas* when an option chain with 60 DTEs is available and let it go to expiration date (with no trade management or any filter added to support decision to open trades). The results below present the average percentage return of this trade (buying a VXX put option with 60 DTEs at different *Deltas*).

A. Six-month analysis (July 18–December 18):[5] (1) first three months with low volatility, (2) last three months with increasing and high volatility, (3) total of four trades

A.1. 70 *Delta*: –52%
A.2. 60 *Delta*: –57%
A.3. 50 *Delta*: –54%
A.4. 40 *Delta*: –57%
A.5. 30 *Delta*: –63%

---

[5] Simulation using VXX with backtester from Capital Market Laboratories

B. Five-year analysis (December 13–December 18):[6] (1) majority of time with low volatility, with peaks, (2) total of 31 trades

B.1. 70 *Delta*: 175%
B.2. 60 *Delta*: 229%
B.3. 50 *Delta*: 209%
B.4. 40 *Delta*: 185%
B.5. 30 *Delta*: 235%

Given these results, it is easy to understand that this trade is profitable when there are long periods of low volatility. And this is aligned with what is expected, given the trade characteristics: it is **a trade that considers a period of more than thirty days and is dependent on consistent price decay of VXX**. If the VXX price is in a range or increases, the trade is negative as we saw in the last semester of 2018.

Nevertheless, we can improve the profitability of this trade with proper management by adding a filter to define entry and closing points. As traders, and understanding the negatives and positives of this trade, let's apply some criteria:
1. Open a trade only when there is contango in place (2 percent or more) for the first two months of VIX futures and there is availability of a 60 DTEs option chain (including weeklies), which means markets are calm, with low volatility. In the simulator, we've assumed a proxy having the price below the ten-day moving average.
2. Close the trade if the 30 DTEs point is reached at any profit or loss.[7] Here, *Theta* is penalizing the trade, and we will be better positioned if we enter a new one.
3. Manage the trade at 25 percent, which means closing it at 25 percent either at a profit or loss.
   And the results will be completely different. See the following outputs:

A. Six-month analysis (July 18–December 18):[8] (1) first three months with low volatility, (2) last three months with increasing and high volatility

A.1. 70 *Delta*: 46% (5 wins in 7 trades)

---

[6] Simulation using VXX with backtester from Capital Market Laboratories

[7] This trade management rule was not considered in the backtester as it does not allow to add this restriction. Therefore, it is fair to assume that the outputs stated are under-estimated, which are good for conservative purposes of the analysis.

[8] Simulation using VXX with backtester from Capital Market Laboratories

A.2. 60 *Delta*: 18% (4 wins in 8 trades)
A.3. 50 *Delta*: -6% (4 wins in 10 trades)
A.4. 40 *Delta*: 43% (4 wins in 8 trades)
A.5. 30 *Delta*: 48% (4 wins in 9 trades)

B. Three-year analysis (December 15–December 18):[9] (1) majority of time with low volatility with periods of high volatility, (2) total of 43–92 trades

B.1. 70 *Delta*: 210% (67% winners)
B.2. 60 *Delta*: 222% (63% winners)
A.3. 50 *Delta*: 247% (63% winners)
B.4. 40 *Delta*: 416% (64% winners)
B.5. 30 *Delta*: 474% (59% winners)

C. Five-year analysis (December 13–December 18):[10] (1) majority of time with low volatility, with peaks, (2) total of 75–161 trades

C.1. 70 *Delta*: 172% (61% winners)
C.2. 60 *Delta*: 166% (58% winners)
C.3. 50 *Delta*: 117% (57% winners)
C.4. 40 *Delta*: 113% (54% winners)
C.5. 30 *Delta*: 225% (54% winners)

Given this new approach, we have turned the initial not profitable trade into a profitable strategy, using proper entry conditions (when there is any volatility increase or it's at high level, wait on the sidelines) and trade management at 25 percent. The best put option to choose, which gives more **consistent results, is at 30 *Delta***. Also, this is in line with what to expect, as this trade doesn't get any better with time, and that's why it makes sense to **manage it with "only" 25 percent of maximum profit or loss, or even close it with a limit of 30 DTEs.** Such development is also expected, as this lower *Delta* put will benefit from increasing *Gamma* as VXX decreases in price, which benefits that option price.

The exact guidelines of entering and managing the trade along with the described strategies are summarized in the following chapters.

---

[9] Simulation using VXX with backtester from Capital Market Laboratories
[10] Simulation using VXX with backtester from Capital Market Laboratories

11

The Hedged VXXB Short Call Vertical

If you have three successive losing trades, it doesn't mean the strategy is wrong. Always aim for the long term.

Core Strategy Introduction

This is where trading volatility with options began for me. It is very profitable when market conditions are ideal—the higher **contango** (in VIX futures structure) the better, and VXXB loses value as time passes due to this effect. But when volatility expands, VXXB can lose value very fast. I call it "hedged" short vertical, because, when I started to trade this strategy, I had several scary moments when volatility increased and that produced bad results for this trade. The natural evolution for this highly profitable trade is to always have some kind of hedging technique prepared to be launched to protect losses from volatility explosions. We'll discuss it later in this chapter.

In fact, this is a *Delta* trade and, hence, a directional play. A short call vertical is the combination of two calls (one sold and another bought in the same ratio): selling a call near-the-money and buying another call out-of-the-money for protection. Depending on the combination of both calls, *Theta* can be positive or negative as well as the number of days to expiration of options. I prefer to use calls, instead of puts (buying put spread vertical will have the same profile) with VXXB, because there are no dividends in this asset. As referred, another construction of the same profile could be using put options. But in this case, we would be buying the vertical: (1)

buying one option in-the-money and (2) selling it near-the-money. But in this case, you aren't collecting premium as selling the vertical with calls (but also at the expense of buying power to cover for full loss on the trade). I won't go into many details about the possibilities of vertical construction. Rather, I'll focus on the juice of this applied strategy to VXXB. What is the best combination of sold/bought call options (which *Delta*?), and what is the timeframe that produces the best results (which DTE?) in the long term?

Fig. 11.1 – Short call vertical illustration for VXXB at 17 DTEs (sold 70 *Delta* / bought 30 *Delta*) entered on January 8, 2019; sold call at 40.5 strike price and bought call at 46.5 strike price. This trade resulted in a credit of US$250 in the brokerage account (also maximum profit) for a US$600 in buying power reduction. Given the current high implied volatility on VXXB options, this credit received is higher than usual, when contango is in place. It's common to have an average credit between 0.8 to 1.2, which means lower profit zone and higher loosing area (above price entered)—lower risk/reward than the current market environment.

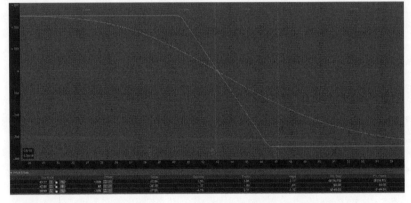

Analyzing the above figure, we can conclude the *Delta* value or directional play of this strategy: *Delta* is negative in the value of 38. This means that this strategy has the same outcome (with all other variables being constant) of shorting 38 units of VXXB stock. *Theta* is roughly null at this time and VXXB price level, as well as *Vega*. Also, we can see that if the price happens to change by 10 percent during the day (which is possible), this trade will lose US$156 and *Theta* will become negative. And the new VXXB price position makes our trade lose value as time passes, and we are simulating with only 17 DTEs (where time decay is high). Risky trade! But if VXXB price decreases, we have all the positives: positive return and *Theta* positive!

Fig. 11.2 – Short call vertical illustration for VXXB from the figure above but simulated at 8 DTEs.

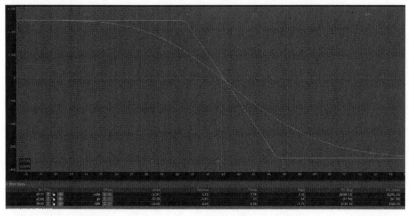

Comparing both figures (one at 17 DTEs and another at 8 DTEs) and the same VXXB price (US$42.88), we note the increase of *Delta* in value (in absolute return)—from 38 to 53, both negative. You can see the increase in steepness of the t0 line (magenta) in the second figure. (*Gamma* increases as we approach the expiry date of the options). If VXXB increased by 10 percent during this period, the loss would be not US$156 but US$206. This is mainly due to time erosion of the bought call. On the contrary, if the market moved in our favor (VXXB decreased in value)—let's assume by 10 percent—then the gain would be US$184. To compare, based on the first figure, it would be "only" US$146. This time, *Theta* and *Delta* played in our favor.

Such a short timeframe example was chosen to illustrate the high risk of this trade, what the forces in play are, and the importance of having a hedging technique along with this trade, but also because this timeframe is, in fact, the trade that I have applied with success to VXX for so long.

Only for your comparison, the figure below illustrates the same trade (short call vertical at 70/30 *Delta*) but at 45 DTEs. The main differences are: lower *Delta* (lower steepness of t0 line—magenta) and bigger amount of credit collected (US$450) but also bigger amount of buying power reduction (US$1,150).

Fig. 11.3 – Short call vertical at 45 DTEs with (70/30 *Delta*).

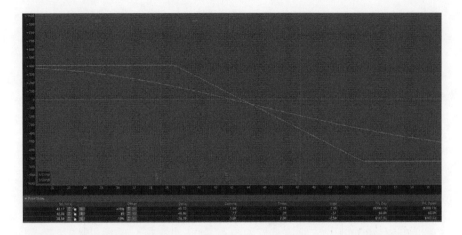

Fig. 11.4 – Illustration of a lower-volatility environment for VXXB short call vertical with lower credit received.

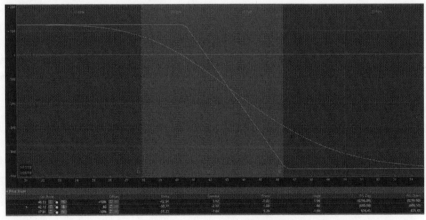

Usually, I don't enter a trade when the credit received is below 0.75. The risk/reward ratio isn't attractive enough. See the comparison of the left side (profit area) v. the right side (losing area) of the graph.

Strategy Development and

Optimization

When I started the process of developing an options strategy that fitted the behavior of VXX price movement, I was looking for a profitable and actionable trade setup to sell volatility with limited risk. It needed to be this way. Shorting the stock directly wasn't an option, as there is unlimited risk in case of volatility explosion. And the early days of February 2018 were one of those periods that could have produced huge losses if that type of strategy were in place. That's why I needed to find a solution with options that allow a more flexible risk management and design. A single put like the one described above has negative *Theta*, which makes me feel a bit uncomfortable. So the vertical option suits me and if applied to VXX has negative price bias. In fact, this strategy is very good when applied with the right market conditions (calm markets with **contango** in play), and VXX has a nice headwind and the price sustainably decreases. But when markets start to move fast to the downside and volatility increases rapidly, this strategy loses big time. That's why it's important to hedge!

During my development process, I started by understanding which timeframe would produce the best results, using the backtesting software.[11] I experimented with seven, fifteen, thirty, and sixty days. And the most consistent and profitable timeframe was fifteen days. Every week, when an options chain with that DTE was available, a new trade was entered. No filter (like contango) or money management was implemented. Below are the simulations for different time horizons with the return percentage:

A. Five-year analysis (December 13–Dec 18): (1) majority of time with low volatility, with peaks, (2) total of 123–136 trades

    A.1. 70/40 *Deltas*: 638% (65% winners)
    A.2. 70/30 *Deltas*: 628% (70% winners)
    A.3. 60/30 *Deltas*: 507% (73% winners)
    A.4. 50/30 *Deltas*: 299% (77% winners)
    A.4. 50/20 *Deltas*: 153% (78% winners)

B. Three-year analysis (December 15–December 18): (1) majority of time with low volatility with periods of high volatility, (2) total of 74–80 trades
    B.1. 70/40 *Deltas*: 171% (65% winners)

    B.2. 70/30 *Deltas*: 195% (71% winners)

---

[11] Simulation using VXX with backtester from Capital Market Laboratories

B.3. 60/30 *Deltas*: 168% (73% winners)
B.4. 50/30 *Deltas*: 208% (78% winners)
B.4. 50/20 *Deltas*: 139% (80% winners)

C. Six-month analysis (July 18–December 18): (1) first three months with low volatility; last three months with increasing and high volatility, (2) total of 13 trades
B.1. 70/40 *Deltas*: -90% (46% winners)
B.2. 70/30 *Deltas*: -97% (46% winners)
B.3. 60/30 *Deltas*: -82% (54% winners)
B.4. 50/30 *Deltas*: -80% (54% winners)
B.4. 50/20 *Deltas*: -71% (54% winners)

From this summary, we can conclude that this strategy doesn't work in choppy markets! It produced negative returns in the last six months, where the market had increased volatility (above average) for a relatively long period (three months). In fact, I haven't been trading this strategy for a while (four months now, as backwardation is still in place). All those simulations included opening trades under non-optimal market conditions and leaving them open until expiry. Again, if we enter proper money management into this simulation, the results will be different. Since backtesting has its limitations regarding the contango filter (i.e., open this short call vertical only when contango is above a certain level, let's say 5 percent), all the below returns can be further improved. Hence, they are underestimated under the proposed trade plan.

Here are the updated simulations with **money management at 50 percent level:** Close the trade when a 50 percent profit or loss point is reached on each trade):

A. Five-year analysis (December 13–December 18): (1) majority of time with low volatility, with peaks, (2) total of 245–266 trades
A.1. 70/40 *Deltas*: 568% (57% winners)
A.2. 70/30 *Deltas*: 735% (59% winners)
A.3. 60/30 *Deltas*: 534% (61% winners)
A.4. 50/30 *Deltas*: 330% (62% winners)
A.4. 50/20 *Deltas*: 484% (64% winners)

B. Three-year analysis (December 15–December 18): (1) majority of time with low volatility with periods of high volatility, (2) total of 140–184 trades
B.1. 70/40 *Deltas*: 210% (61% winners)
B.2. 70/30 *Deltas*: 240% (61% winners)
B.3. 60/30 *Deltas*: 190% (64% winners)

B.4. 50/30 *Deltas*: 149% (65% winners)

B.4. 50/20 *Deltas*: 176% (66% winners)

C. Six-month analysis (July 18–December 18) isn't computed, as it produced, again, negative returns (higher than the above six-month simulation without money management) for all combinations due to higher volatility period and not being possible to simulate contango effect as a filter to open trades.

Clearly, the best combination, or the one that produces the best return, for the **15-day short call vertical is selling the 70 *Delta* call and buying the 30 *Delta* call. It is capable of delivering very high returns** (higher than the ones stated above if only entered when market is in contango).

To sum up, we can implement this strategy, trading with proper management and adding a filter to define entry and closing points:

1. Evaluate VIX futures contango level for the first two months.
2. If contango level is above 3 percent, a trade can be opened if there is availability of VXXB option chain of 14–17 DTEs (it could include weeklies), meaning markets are calm /low volatility in place, and credit received is above 0.75.
3. Close the trade if, either profit or loss, reaches 50 percent of the initial credit received, i.e., if the price of the sold vertical was US$1.00, close it if it reaches US$0.5 (at a profit) or US$1.50 (at a loss).

Hedging Technique

Due to relatively high risk of this strategy, it is advisable to use some of its high profitability to offset losses due to volatility explosions. I never trade this short vertical without any hedging (sometimes I can assume this risk if contango level is above 10 percent and not in the last two–three days of the front month VIX future expiration). However, most of the time (let's say 90 percent), I am hedged. It softens both the losses and the profits. But I don't care if this strategy can deliver such high returns! I can spare a fraction of it on insurance! There were times when I was too greedy and didn't use it, with bad consequences. That's why, I am always hedged when I have this strategy in place. We never know what market is preparing for us. Even on a weekend, some event could occur, and VXXB would gap up. So why have avoidable losses if we can position ourselves better?

My preferred hedging technique is using VIX calls—not exactly buying one call, but buying a vertical (buying a call above the spot VIX level and selling another VIX call four or five strike prices above) with 30-45 DTEs. For example, if spot VIX sat around 13, I would choose to buy 15 call and selling another call at 20. The maximum price to pay for this vertical shouldn't exceed 1.0. Usually, I keep it around 0.80. At current volatility conditions with VIX at 20.55, I would buy a 22/26 vertical for 0.80 debit—see the figure below.

Fig. 11.5 – VIX call spread illustration with market conditions on January 8, 2019

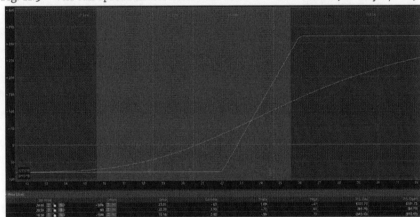

Let me highlight that VIX options refer to the correspondent expiry future and not to spot VIX. This means that this vertical spread reacts slower than you could expect because VIX futures also react slower to volatility variations than the VIX itself (this was discussed in the previous chapter).

One good property of VIX options that make this trade attractive (risk/reward profile) is about volatility skew on VIX calls. If you analyze the implied volatility of VIX calls, you will understand that the implied volatility increases as we move along the strike prices. See the yellow box in the image below.

Fig. 11.6 – Option chain for VIX at 35 DTEs highlighting implied volatility, with spot VIX being at 20.89 and VIX future with maturity in thirty-five days at 20.95.

		CALLS				Strikes: ALL		
Impl Vol	Delta	Open Int	Volume	Bid X	Ask X		Exp	Strike
▼ 13 FEB 19 (35) :00 (Weeklys)								
78.64%	.99	186	0				13 FEB 19	12
70.72%	.99	0	0	3.50 C			13 FEB 19	12.5
64.99%	.99	513	0				13 FEB 19	13
59.85%	.99	0	4				13 FEB 19	13.5
54.40%	.99	151	1				13 FEB 19	14
49.17%	.99	0	0				13 FEB 19	14.5
68.46%	.95	1,043	0				13 FEB 19	15
68.93%	.91	36,159	0				13 FEB 19	16
71.26%	.85	7,550	56				13 FEB 19	17
73.87%	.78	11,238	12				13 FEB 19	18
74.22%	.70	14,905	1				13 FEB 19	19
75.07%	.62	75,902	4				13 FEB 19	20
78.35%	.54	19,090	142	1.95 C	2.05 C		13 FEB 19	21
79.53%	.47	26,991	90	1.60 C	1.65 C		13 FEB 19	22
82.97%	.61	28,130	236	1.35 C	1.40 C		13 FEB 19	23
84.25%	.35	47,579	2	1.10 C	1.15 C		13 FEB 19	24
85.66%	.30	36,934	20,040	.95 C	.95 C		13 FEB 19	25
88.31%	.26	14,871	15	.75 C	.80 C		13 FEB 19	26
90.66%	.22	62,233	11	.65 C	.70 C		13 FEB 19	27
92.58%	.19	43,134	2	.55 C	.60 C		13 FEB 19	28
94.09%	.17	15,826	0	.45 C	.55 C		13 FEB 19	29
96.22%	.15	91,234	260	.40 C	.45 C		13 FEB 19	30
102.58%	.11	41,837	5	.30 C	.35 C		13 FEB 19	32.5
105.19%	.08	141,497	0	.20 C	.25 C		13 FEB 19	35
112.61%	.07	328,229	0	.15 C	.25 C		13 FEB 19	37.5
115.30%	.05	183,381	0	.10 C	.20 C		13 FEB 19	40
119.60%	.04	58,019	0	.10 C	.15 C		13 FEB 19	42.5
126.90%	.04	91,504	24	.10 C	.15 C		13 FEB 19	45
129.28%	.03	23,441	0	.05 C	.15 C		13 FEB 19	47.5
129.90%	.03	38,341	0	.80 C	.10 C		13 FEB 19	50
141.10%	.02	26,501	0	.05 C	.10 C		13 FEB 19	

But how to combine the short call 70/30 vertical with this hedging technique? Hedging means insurance, and if we were willing to have full hedging, all the losses from the main trade would be offset by the hedging part of the trade. Otherwise, we would have a free lunch. So, my advice is to have one VIX call spread per two VXXB short call verticals—i.e., a hedging ratio of 2:1. Bear in mind that this hedging trade loses money as time passes (in normal market conditions) due to *Theta* decay and roll yield. You shouldn't have this trade in place in the last twenty days before expiration. Close trade and add a new one, better positioned for current market environment. Also, when it loses 40 percent–50 percent of its value, I close it and add another trade. (Usually, when the vertical reaches 0.5 value, I close it). Don't stick to it until the expiry point!

Another issue that is very important to take into consideration is losing on the VXXB short vertical and winning on the VIX vertical. When it happens, don't remove the hedge and keep the main trade, expecting the volatility to retract and let you win in both trades. Don't make this rookie mistake. Always remove them at the same moment!

The short VXXB call vertical is a risky trade, and I advise you to always protect it with a hedge!

12

The Creative VXXB Unbalanced Iron Condor

For each opened trade, define your exit points: both at gain and loss!

Strategy Background and Properties

During the last months of 2017 and beginning of 2018, my applying the short call vertical strategy turned out to be highly profitable; markets were moving high, with very low volatility and high levels of contango. Then, came the big volatility spike in February 2018, and I was glad to have my hedges in place. Nevertheless, I suffered some losses that could have been big if the hedges hadn't been there! That's why I always reinforce the importance of having hedges in place and avoiding big losses—especially during those unexpected volatility explosions. The probability of their occurring is low, but sometimes they do happen. Until May, **contango** wasn't present, and I was on the sidelines; market was choppy, and VIX ranged between 15 and 26. During this period, I was intrigued and thought about designing a new volatility-based strategy to use VXX or other volatility ETN that could be profitable under high volatility periods (and high implied volatility from VXX options) as well, with backwardation in VIX futures, and be present in the market. After several tests and more inspiration from some existing index options strategies that I had researched in my trading past (using broken wing butterflies), I came up with a hypothesis of developing a strategy that would protect from volatility expansions, capture VXX expected price decay, and also benefit from options time decay (*Theta* positive). The "creative" unbalanced iron condor (UIC) was born! I called it the

"Croc" trade, as it resembles the head of a croc with the eyes above water and the nose on the surface (cyan line—expiry date in the figure below). Fig. ?? illustrates the profile of the trade that is a combination of put and call vertical spreads, unbalanced in quantities and strike prices, using a higher timeframe (60–70 DTEs) than the short call vertical spread (70/30) (see the previous chapter).

Fig. 12.1 – "Croc" trade profile using VXXB entered on January 9, 2019 (65 DTEs), revamped from the initial version where the far right short call vertical didn't exist, and added to increase profitability and reduce overall *Delta*.

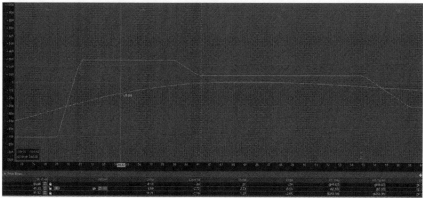

The main characteristics of the "Croc" trade are as follows:

1. Limited risk on the upside – self-hedged against sudden volatility spikes, with plenty of space to adjust the trade in case of volatility increase; In the example above, if VXX increased by 10 percent, the trade could gain a bit (but due to expected increase in implied volatility of VXX options, it could be null). This trade should have a slightly positive *Delta* for most of its existence. You can see a positive slope in t0 line (magenta) at the price entered (41.23).

2. Controlled risk on the downside – The short put vertical (29/31) makes this trade with limited risk to be also on the downside, but at risk higher than on the upside. Given the VXX price properties, we know that the violent moves are more related to volatility explosions (to the upside), and hence, assuming this extra risk presents no big issues. VXXB has a slower price movement to the downside, which is manageable.

3. Benefits from VXXB price decay (due to roll yield and contango) – As you can understand from the structure of this complex options positions, the head of the "croc" sits where there is more probability for the VXXB to land near the expiration point, which is a higher profit zone.

4. Benefits from options time decay (*Theta* positive) – The presented options structure consists of options selling (vertical spreads) and, hence, gives positive *Theta*.

5. *Vega* negative – The presented structure, composed of options selling, has high sensitivity to implied volatility of VXXB options, with an inverse relation. This means that when the options' volatility increases, there is a negative impact on the price of the structure. That is why, I recommend that this structure should be kept with slightly positive *Delta* as a hedge against volatility. This *Vega* negative property is good to protect against volatility drop in the market and implied volatility drop in VXXB options. This is highly important when the trade is entered when VXXB volatility is high and it starts to drop as well as VXX price. It delivers a buffer against *Delta*.

6. Lower *Delta* sensitivity / *Delta* neutral – In comparison with the other described trades, this one has the lower *Delta* sensitivity. As you can see from the figure above, the t0 line (magenta) is quite flat.

7. High profit range area – In the given example, the range of the profit this trade would bring in at the point when VXXB expires is between 31 and 55. This means that a probability of this trade to be profitable is around 80 percent. Note that the higher profit zone (US$300) is on the left (the head of the "croc"), where there is more probability of VXXB to land, while the lower profit zone (US$100) is between 41 and 55 (where the nose of the "croc" is).

Description

The "Croc" trade can be opened without being concerned about the VIX futures curve structure. It can be opened at any moment, given the availability of an option chain between 60 and 70 DTEs. The use of *Delta* to determine strikes is another way of defining a trade structure, and it adjusts according to market conditions. Also, it is better to control total *Delta*. I prefer to use monthly chains and not weeklies for this trade. The traded is defined by opening three verticals with the following characteristics (for one lot):

(A) Short put vertical (left side): **five units** with the short put to be entered at **10** *Delta*; the long put to be bought **two strikes below** (in the example given is 29/31);

(B) Short call vertical (right side): **one unit** with the short call being at **20** *Delta* and the bought call at **15** *Delta*;

(C) Short call vertical (middle): **one unit** with the short call being at **65** *Delta* and the bought Call **two strikes above**;

(D) The Buying Power Reduction (BPR) for one lot trade *circa* US$1,000, given the verticals structure, credits received and market conditions.

Trade Dynamics

The rationale of this trade is to have in our favor the options time decay that go along with the VXXB time decay and land on the head just before expiration. This type of trade is also not to be left until expiration. Usually, I don't have it in place it below 20 DTEs. After this day, *Gamma* is high, and it's better to close the trade, take out profits (or losses), and enter a new better-positioned trade.

The following figures illustrate the evolution of the trade with the passage of time (maintaining implied volatility constant) and help better understand its dynamics. Focus on the t0 line that represents the structure of the trade at each given moment. The cyan line is the profile at expiration.

Fig 12.2 – Simulation of the trade entered on January 9, 2019, thirty days later on February 9, 2019 (35 DTEs).

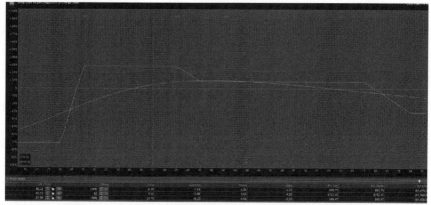

The main difference to note is the growth of a "bubble" due to options price decay of *Theta*. At this moment, the trade can be profitable if VXXB price is between the small red marks (35 and 52). If the price after thirty days is around the current price (41), we are at the top of t0 line, and *Delta* is flat (3). If VXXB decays in price and sits, for example, at 37 (decay of 10 percent of the current price), the trade is still positive and *Delta* is fairly positive (24), with *Theta* being at 4.8. This means that the *Delta/Theta* ratio is roughly 5. This isn't too much for this trade, but we will describe adjustments later. On the other side, if VXXB price increases by 10 percent (to 45.22), *Delta* becomes negative and *Theta* decreases, because it is far from the "Croc" head that gives a boost in *Theta* decay, but the trade is still positive.

Fig 12.3 – Simulation of the trade entered on January 9, 2019, forty days later on February 19, 2019 (25DTEs).

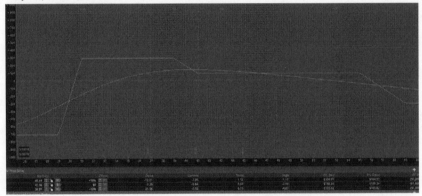

Going further in time, *Theta* decay will increase, as expected, and the profitability range will also expand. The top of the bulge (where *Delta* is null) reduced from 41 to 40 is seen on the t0 line of the above figure.

As you may conclude from the trade structure, the bulge moves along the expected VXXB price decay. This type of trade isn't so demanding when it comes to daily monitoring the short call vertical (70/30). It is calmer, less risky, and more reliable (it has higher statistical probability of achieving positive trades). With it, also come lower expected returns. For one lot of this trade, expect to earn around circa 100USD. Which for an investment of 1000USD in one month is very good!

The worst situation, when it's hard for this trade to become profitable, is when there is a huge drop in VXXB price after *Theta* decay kicks in, and the implied volatility reduction (*Vega* negative) isn't capable of absorbing this rapid movement. Another situation (with a low probability of occurrence) is a huge explosion of volatility with the VXXB price creating a gap of 20 percent and huge increase in implied volatility of VXXB options where the short call spread at higher strike prices becomes almost reached. As mentioned, the steady increase in VXXB price can be a good thing and would give time to take out the position at a profit. It all depends on the time of the VXXB price movement between the date entered and 20 DTEs, where it isn't advisable to continue with this trade opened.

Adjustments and Target Return

Most option trades with a longer timeframe (15–90 DTEs) require some adjustments because time is passing, affecting not only all the Greeks but also price movements on the asset. This options structure is no different. Due to the complexity of this trade, there are several adjustments to consider, and they are a bit more complex than the other trades presented in this book. But before going into detail of the several adjustments of this trade, let's focus on the target return for this type of trade, as it is one of the rules to close it. The target profit of this trade is 10 percent of the total BPR. Given this is roughly a US$1,000 investment in this trade, you should close it if this target is reached (roughly around US$100 per lot). I wouldn't define a clear loss value as the adjustments protect the account and a similar maximum loss value could be expected. Additionally, to properly understand the adjustments and how they are made, we need to classify two time zones that will impact how the adjustment is made:

Zone (1): from entry until 45 DTEs – lower *Theta* decay. To consider adjustments.

Zone (2) from 44 until 20 DTEs — higher *Theta* decay. At this zone, it is better to reposition the whole structure and not to make any adjustments.

A. Lower short put vertical (A) — left side

A.1. Zone (1): When short put reaches 30 *Delta*, buy the short put and sell the immediate lower strike (the short vertical will become with 1 strike difference, instead of 2);

A.2. Zone (2): When short put reaches 30 *Delta*, **close the entire position**. Wait for another option cycle.

B. Upper short call vertical (B) – right side

B.1. Zone (1) – If the short call reaches 30 *Delta*, close position and enter a new one, using the same option chain;

B.2. Zone (2) – If the short call reaches 30 *Delta*, close this vertical and open a new one at strikes with 20/15 *Delta* (short 20/long 15).

B.3. Whenever the short call reaches 10 *Delta*, close this vertical and open a new one at 20/15 *Delta*. This will take out some profit and lower *Delta*.

C. Middle short call vertical (C) – middle

B.1. Zone (1) – Close vertical when *Delta* of the short call reaches 45 and enter a new two-strike interval vertical with short call at 65 *Delta*. This will lower *Delta* and take out profit of this vertical.

Trade exits to be considered at one of each alternatives below:

1. Profit target reached: at 10 percent of BPR (usually around US$100 per lot)
2. When 20 DTEs are reached
3. Point A.2. above (adjustments)

Since this trade has several verticals in it and can give you profits before you have to pay broker commissions, I advise to use a discount broker. There are some good brokerage firms with below-average commissions. I moved to Tastyworks, which charges US$1 per leg to open a trade and no commission to close. Also, they offer capped commissions for more than ten contracts per leg. This trade will benefit strongly from a brokerage firm charging low commissions.

13

Putting It all Together: Portfolio Risk Management

The consistent trader constantly manages their overall positions risk, not trying to achieve their target return!

Portfolio Management

After the description of each individual trade strategy, let's discuss a bit further and have a properly combined **Trade Plan**. As you probably know, I am a bit conservative as a trader and always look at my Greeks before entering a new trade. What will be the impact of adding a new trade to my overall portfolio in terms of *Delta*, *Theta* and *Vega*? Do I need to adjust current trades? If I close a trade, what will be the impact? Do I need to enter a new trade? I never enter new positions without evaluating the potential impact on the portfolio.

Usually, if markets are calm and contango is present, I have in play two batches of short call verticals with one-week difference, which give me negative *Delta* and slightly positive *Theta* (i.e., the week n-1 trade and the current week trade) and their respective *Delta* hedges (VIX call verticals). Additionally, I have two longer-dated trades (unbalanced iron condors, also with different expiration dates) to add positive *Theta* and also some positive *Delta* to the overall portfolio. To sum up, two sets of short call verticals and two sets of unbalanced iron condors—all trades with different expirations, which is good in terms of risk diversification. I tend not to use the other *Delta* negative trade (long put), not to increase complexity of my positions, and not to have too much negative *Delta*.

Under calm market conditions, low volatility (VIX<14), the short call verticals play the biggest role in producing returns. The UIC (unbalanced iron condors) have lower profitability. Usually, my account accelerates profits during these periods. I prefer to have the short call vertical as the main strategy for producing negative *Delta* if contango is present. Also, as explained, it gives nice returns when market conditions are good. To sum up, during these periods, the short call vertical is my main strategy, and the UIC works like a *Delta* and *Theta* hedge. Sometimes, the latter can produce negative return, but I don't care, as I have a total positive return overall (including paying for the VIX hedges).

When volatility is high (VIX>15), usually backwardation or a small contango is present. This isn't good for the short call vertical, and this strategy isn't traded (as per its trade plan). This is a good environment for the UIC, especially, if also VXXB implied volatility is high. The strike selection gives a wider structure, with positive *Theta* and *Delta* that should be monitored closely not to move outside a fair range. I prefer to have a slightly positive *Delta* in this market environment to be protected from volatility spikes. After huge volatility explosions, like the ones in August 2015, February 2018, or October 2018, volatility retractions last for two–four months to get back to normal levels. So when volatility retracts, the UIC benefits from implied volatility reduction in VXXB options, which smoothens eventual losses not compensated by time decay, as *Delta* is positive (with the trade being loose when VXXB retracts).

As you can conclude, all these trades ought to be balanced in order to manage mainly directional risk (*Delta*) and time decay (*Theta*). I don't recommend adding short call verticals if *Delta* is already negative enough! Even if there is nice amount of contango (e.g., above 10 percent), we never know what the market will do the next day, night, or even during a weekend. Don't take excessive risks! Always evaluate the impact any additional trade has on Greeks, think of an adjustment, or close the trade.

Account Management

Following the above discussion about portfolio management, I would like to add some simple final thoughts on account management, which I learned from my experience: Greed is the enemy of a consistent trader! Again, I learned the wrong way. During the periods of getting huge gains, I reinvested those gains in added positions, expecting the lovely effect of compounding returns. Mistake. When there was a volatility spike, the positions were negative, and the losses kicked in, the compounding effect also entered the equation!

My answer to this effect is to consider certain capital that you are using to trade. Let's say you allocate to your trading US$10,000. This is your asset. Over this, you should produce a certain monthly return. Every month that you have in your account a value in excess of your capital, you should take it out or not trade it. I suggest you withdraw it in order to resist the temptation. Also, you'll start benefiting from your profits and, in fact, start to see them! I think this is a wise approach to avoid greed.

The Trader Commandments

Always be prepared for the unexpected!

Don't add another similar trade to a losing position.

Volatility is elastic! Know how to play with it.

Volatility takes the stairs down but the elevator up!

If you expect the market to move one way, it'll probably move the other.

If you expect to earn 20 percent in a trade, consider paying for insurance, i.e., hedge your position.

You won't always be on the winning side!

You are an investor, not a gambler!

When you open a trade, be prepared for the worst. Hedge!

Guessing the market direction is hard! I mostly fail trying to do it.

If you have three successive losing trades, it doesn't mean the strategy is wrong. Always aim for the long term.

For each opened trade, define your exit points: both at gain and loss!

The consistent trader constantly manages their overall positions risk, not trying to achieve their target return!

The Volatility Trade Plan

I decided to create a chapter focused on a Trade Plan for each strategy, which you can easily follow or even print to have it at your hands in order to check whether you need to remember the guidelines of each trade. Let me also remind that these guidelines are focused on trading independently and not as an overall portfolio of presented VXXB trades. This means that you should take into consideration, when entering a trade, what the risk of your current portfolio is and what the impact of a new trade to it is. Does it flatten *Delta*? Do you increase your overall *Theta*? And what about your *Vega* risk? These are several questions you need to ask when you have already opened positions and you are willing to add another one, even if conditions are met to enter a new trade! Beware that trading is risk management! Not gambling.

The Easiest Volatility Options Strategy

Open Trade Conditions

1. Contango level > 2%
2. VXXB price below 10 Day Simple Moving Average
3. Availability of an option chain with 57-63 DTE

Closing Trade conditions

1. Profit or Loss of 25% reached (from entry cost)*
2. 30 DTE reached

*If cost of a single Put is 3.00USD (300 USD maximum risk for 100 shares), the price target of the option is 3.75USD and Max loss when price reach 2.25)

The Hedged VXXB Short Call Vertical

Open Trades Conditions

1. Contango level > 3%
2. Availability of an option chain with 14-17 DTE
3. Open both:
    1. 2 VXXB Short Calls Spread @ 70/30 Deltas with 14-17 DTE
        - Credit received > 0.75 (per spread)
    2. 1 Long Call Vertical on VIX with 30-45 DTE
        - Long Call 2 strikes above spot VIX / Short Call 4-5 strikes above
        - Debit paid between 0.8 and 1.0

Closing Trades conditions

1. Profit or Loss of 50% reached (based on credit received at open)*
2. 5 DTE reached
3. Close also the hedge trade (VIX Vertical) when VXXB be trade is closed

*If credit received is 1.00 the price target will be 1.50 and maximum price at max loss is 0.50

The Creative VXXB Unbalanced Iron Condor

Open Trade Conditions

---

1. Availability of an option chain with 60-70 DTE
2. (A) Short Put Vertical (5 units) @ 10 Delta Put / 2 Strikes below
3. (B) Short Call Vertical (1 unit) @ 20/15 Delta
4. (C)Short Call Vertical (1 unit) @ 65 Delta Call / 2 strikes above

---

Adjustments

Zone (1): DTE > 45

1. (A) Short Put reach 30 Delta: buy the short Put and sell the immediate lower strike
2. (B) Short Call reach 30 Delta: close entire position and open a new one with same option chain
3. (B) Whenever Short Call reach 10 Delta, close Vertical and open a new one @ 20 / 15 Delta
4. (C) When Short Call reach 45, close Vertical and open a new one @ 65 Delta / 2 strikes above

Zone (2) DTE < 45 (until 20 DTE)

1. (A) Short Put reach 30 Delta: close entire position
2. (B) Short Call reach 30 Delta: close this Vertical and open a new one @ 20/15 Delta
3. (B) Whenever Short Call reach 10 Delta, close Vertical and open a new one @ 20 / 15 Delta

---

Closing Trade conditions

---

1. Profit of 10% reached (based on BPR)
2. 20 DTE reached
3. When Short Put reach 30 Delta at 20 < DTE < 45

16

A Brief on Option Greeks

Delta

Delta is the Greek letter that signifies directional exposure. It can also be used to (1) determine the equivalent number of shares and (2) estimate the probability of the option to expire in the money. In essence, it delivers the rate of change of an option's price, given a $1 increase in the underlying price. **Positive *Delta*** strategies gain if the underlying price increases. In contrast, strategies that have **negative *Delta*** gain if the underlying price decreases. If an option has 20 *Delta*, it means that it has a 16-percent probability to end in-the-money.

***Delta* neutral** strategies or portfolios refer to overall options positions that have a total *Delta* value of about 0 and are fairly neutral to the underlying price movements.

Calls have positive *Deltas*, and puts have negative *Deltas*.

Gamma

Gamma is the Greek letter signifying the rate of change of an option's *Delta*, given a move in the underlying. Long option positions benefit from increasing *Gamma*. As you approach the expiration point, *Gamma* increases, which means *Delta* variations are more pronounced to lower-price movements of the underlying due to the steepness of the probability curve. It can quickly turn winning trades into losing ones and vice versa. It is preferable to avoid these drastic swings, which is the reason not to have open positions five days prior to expiration.

***Gamma* is beneficial to long option holders**. It accelerates profits for every move of the underlying in traders' favor and decelerates losses for every move the underlying goes against. In contrast, *Gamma* is extra-risky for option sellers. From the sellers' perspective, it can accelerate losses and decelerate directional gains.

Theta

Theta signifies the daily decay of an option's extrinsic value, assuming other variables constant. If a position has **positive *Theta***, it will increase value as time passes and is possible only if we sell options. For option sellers, *Theta* decay is a good thing.

If a position has **negative *Theta***, it will lose value as the time passes. Negative *Theta* is achieved when options bought outpace the options sold.

The extrinsic value of options will decrease as we approach expiration, which means we have to be directionally right and quick, or implied volatility to increase in order to see a profit.

Vega

Vega is the Greek letter signifying the value of options given changes in implied volatility. *Vega* values representing the change in an option's price, given a 1 percent move in implied volatility, all else are equal. Long options have **positive *Vega*** and will benefit if implied volatility increases. When option prices are being bid up by people purchasing them, implied volatility increases. When options are being sold, implied volatility will decrease. **Long options positions have a positive *Vega* and short options have a negative *Vega*.** An increase in implied volatility will benefit the long option positions, as that indicates an increase in option prices; hence, the positive *Vega*. On the contrary, a decrease in implied volatility will benefit the short-option holder, as that indicates a decrease in option pricing, hence negative *Vega*.

Made in the USA
Middletown, DE
25 May 2023

31352392R00043